Also by Gail Gauldin Moore from Deerbrook Editions

Daughter of the Rain

Stricken

Gail Gauldin Moore

Poems in the Time of Covid

DEERBROOK EDITIONS

PUBLISHED BY
Deerbrook Editions
P.O. Box 542
Cumberland, ME 04021
www.deerbrookeditions.com
digital catalog previews:
www.issuu.com/deerbrookeditions

FIRST EDITION
© 2022 by Gail Gauldin Moore

ISBN: 978-1-7368477-5-6
Book design by Jeffrey Haste

for Michael

Contents

Part I

Part I

For now we see through a glass, darkly;
but then face to face: now I know in part;
but then shall I know even as also I am known.

I Corinthians 13: 12

I am angry. I want to shake bird from the tree;
Interfere with the absurd run of squirrel.

Inject Clorox into the puerile mind.
Place my body on the runway.

The sky has no lid. There are knots of worry.
Everything is extreme.

> Suppose a Bat infects a Pangolin
> and the world shuts down.

Ignorance bewitches sense altogether
and Evil is an elemental thing.

Systems Management

When I was six, I was a flute.
Later I was many sounds.

When I was the sound of the void,
I was myself.

But I began to wander from
the starting place

and other places did not
become me.

I was alone with oatmeal
and different walls,

but I kept wandering, trying to
find God in his own country.

I wanted him to hide me in
his cowhide vest,

put green apples in my hand,
and declare time—redeemable.

The Blue, Blue Sky

The three pandemics have killed all color.
Maybe there will be a growth of new color.

But I'm wondering if the sky will close.
I thought of the sky as permanent.

Or protective anyway and when I was a child
I sent a letter to God there.

If the sky closes, their will be a protracted disembodiment.
Once things were better. Jersey cow was pleasant to look at.

I miss the scent of yesterday. The seat of my solidity.
Neither mindful nor muttering.

I cannot dream my hero's dream. Can't format my need.
But I honor the depth of your eyes.

Fascist Headlights

No more greater good—sold for cheap.
The darkness spreads and one loses

the territory of the self.
Becomes a person of forced circumstance;

an immense solitary.

The guardian should have come.
The guardians' footprints kept me on a high.

The furniture is askew.
It has been transplanted and does not fit.

The ego rants and sheds its skin.
Truth is pudding, up for grabs.

Re-record.

Continue to include me in the general scheme.
I am still in love with the familiar.

Trace memories of a constant me, demand
I be included in next years little plans.

I don't want to leave with my face unfinished
and my fires put out.

But days crowd each other—stepping stones are slipping.
The ground of being is alarmed.

Running shoes are missing - my promises unsecured.
Heart beats are on alert.

Donnelly vs. Almost Everyone

Once he was light years away
from the sidewalk on Beverly & Fairfax.

Then he was ten.
Now how, at thirty eight,

Was he to be?

His cheeks to shave?
His legs to make—a bold stride forward?

Almost everyone, never noticing what they notice,
walked around.

His silence was absolute—here on the flinty street:
The eyeless street: The poem-less street.

The sullen street, where hapless hours are born.

What about a briefcase full of cause?
Or a blue/green swimming pool? A work week?
Funds for something nice?

Moral intelligence scattered.
No case called Donnelley v. Almost Everyone,
was ever filed.

Being, Eclipsed

Take away this spring which was not spring.
Along with fall which removed the feet of summer.

Take everything that is something other then itself.
I'm tired of taking up room in this circus of impostures.

Before disease and dialectics, there was life.
There was the heart's affairs and keeping up.

There was the single-celled amoeba, crying
for its mother.

Now we are pawns of a rancid and rapacious clown—
shrill and deranged.

We are pallbearers, with discarnate minds, waiting to
shut the spigot off—take this de-creating process down.

*In the cities, the bells rang all day long: everyone was being
summoned, but no one knew who was summoning them or why**

*see end notes

For Men

I'll write about men.

A man's love is after all, fairly spectacular.

I'll remember arms and shoulders more then lips,
which were tentative.

I'll write about a man's heart.

(The heart as metaphor)
As nomenclature for a driving wind or a pubescent sun.

I'll write about men,

who spend years stepping out of their fathers' shadow

to search for pieces of what might be themselves
or whatever supersedes the whole.

Leaves

I was estranged from the leaves
and the breeze that sang them.

They were not exciting when I was young.
It took time to reclaim them.

Now I stand at the edge of something different.
But I remember the long days before life became intermittent.

I am still estranged from the leaves,
but when my eyes begin to look like strawberries

and everything seems strange, their presence
comforts me.

Did I ruin your speech to God?
Did you draw my name between

time past and time present?
Did you choose me as your mother?

And, if what will come, has been already,
how will I know you again, for the first time?

What is the sense of going back and forth,
if not to find the still point?

Then is the search over?
Or will it close in the ordinary?

At an office supply store
or wearing a frayed slipper?

The Body As Sadist

For nine months my body was *their* body.
Sometimes my body was a great, Hurrah!.

Lately, surreptitious organs are having a childish fight.
Brawling in face: Breaking boundaries.

Something is grabbing the heart: Holding it in an angry grip.
The lungs are weeping.

A trial by fire is this rebellion by the body.
Everything is bated: Still-born: Meatless: Merciless:

The whole that held the parts is letting go.

It's strange how much we pampered the body
to comfort the Soul. But an emptiness remained.

The body has always succumbed to its provisional nature.

Was this a blotched job from the beginning?
No! The mind suffered so the body cried out.

Now with no body and no mind, what was the whole?

A sound perhaps:
Like a Rams horn. Or the chime of bells in a distant place.

Justice Jettisoned

This is for you
        A leaf in the wind

Once you were in place
        A welcome permanence

Before truth burned bridges
        and made hard copies of the lie

I was mostly ego
        Derivative/supplemental

Multiplied by points of reference
        Now I am undersized

Wound-weary
        harpooned by pity and fear

Once justice had a human heart—pity a human face.*

*Anon.

Death

Who are you?
Lurking in the nave between space and time.

Wedging yourself between me and long- term plans.
Calling me your de- flowered concubine.

Nascent forager into the hearts hope;
Traitor to my penchant for the ordinary.

What are you?
I have heard it said that you are an enemy

until your kiss makes you a friend.

Eighty one years have passed since I was
lightening and you were the sky.

That was before time took over.

Why is everything so different?

I cannot find my mirages and I suffer.

I wanted to add up to something that made sense.

Only that which can do a cartwheel in its own shadow,
can relieve me.

You! now loose and full of silver, where are you going
with your extraordinary wing span?

Your pockets full of lessons and ripe fruit?

As you were all right,
I ordered the small rug, I ordered the chair, the store the sheets,
the other rug. I ordered the last towel.

I'll keep up
though the news is bad.

You are a faceless flower
and I am a dark shoe.

Orange men are taking over.
Here at home friends send regrets.

And I lost my last Angel,
the one with the broken tooth.

That Angel could make memories out of ash.
He could create primary colors in the dark.

He could push—back
in a blue suit, holding a hot cup.

Promises build up while
the universe writes an appeal.

Mind is to shackle, what heart is to fear.

Places

I wanted to write to you but nothing I write has wings.
I live in a place without wings.

This page itself, is as dead bird.
You are in a place without wings and few quiet memories.

You'd think that in the thick of things,
God would have given us that—quietude and wings.

But months came, full of sea gulls.
Life became a lesson in case management.

Living Largely

I want to be

Somebody's good news,
live in the light of yesterdays intention.

Yesterday had a green thumb
and planted new worlds.

It ignored the carpies of the mind, who said:
Love without loving: Hope without hoping

and thereby emptied the town of substance.

Now the tawdry and the commonplace lay at my feet.
Bottom fish circle the square.

I do not like carports or chair yoga,
strategies for successful aging.

I like wholehearted welcomes.
I like the Willow not the Palm.

Reading Glasses

I call reading glasses intimate apparel.
I call them a life form.

Your glasses extended you outward.
You had them made to fit your hope,

Why didn't anyone really know you?
Where is the face Christ sent?

Is this a step upward?
Can you touch the sky?

You had them made to fit your hope.
Don't you remember?

Short Sightedness

It has been a long time since we spilled
secrets in the dark and were not separate griefs.

Shy of death, we made a bonfire of our miseries.
But it was not enough to light the underground.

Did you and I shake worlds together?
It would be a mistake to think so.

I could not make a patchwork quilt
with what you gave me.

It was thread bare and did not cover the source.

All in all, it was a merry-go round of effort.
Whirlwinds of complaint sat on every joy,

You were a sword, with a silken edge.
I a formula, divided in half, troubleshooting

in a late hour.

Wanting Certitude

I am tired of making mistakes,
I am tired of announcing my mistakes.

I am tired of hills, mountains, rocks.
Intense is our separation.

The Antelope interests me and the Elephant.

The eyes of crabs interest me,
Though I do not like to look at them,

If I could find my ring with the coral lady's face,
Or you would come to stay, I would be alright.

Changing Horses

Why didn't I know before that there
were answers to the politics of dread?

That Angels flying wingless and backward
should be given the right of way

and enough supporting care
until they knew that everyone

could have their bread buttered
on both sides.

And that there was enough

from each

               accordingly
to each

               accordingly
to teach

            radical holiness?

A Play on Time

I was going.
Just how fast I did not know.

It's all revealed in that play
I am closing as

the outages
are severe and the script unctuous.

But age is a shrinking of absolutes.*

It is not age that matters though.
It is new age with its never, never look.

But to push back would be like
watching butterflies pull on the reins of horses.

I am large in cause, if not in fact, living
In the solitude of curfew and lament.

*Anon

This Morning (Election 2020)

It was easier to be alive; easier
to watch the spirit, entertain the mind.
Easier to be brave again.

Life could be about itself again:
Small deaths resume their place.
We might color in a morning.

Perhaps the restoration has begun.
Perhaps the narrows have given way,
to the possibility of infinite outreach.

Still the wild sirens of the heart.
Make the rivers intentionality your personal story.

You are covered in pleas - a fierce rendering of the caged heart.
Mother madness plummets the silence.

You were the sweet leaf in my dream of sweet.

The smithy in my dream of change.

The tall man in my dream of futures.

I dreamed these dreams over and over again.

I Mother

Forsaking past hope,
garner new dreams.

Show them alternate realities:
Ones that can be absorbed

Into the furniture;
That can be trusted.

I hold you
in the great expanse of being.

And I am drunk on believing
that you will be viable and free,

Knowing Justice

"as the chief and fundamental fact
of your existence."*

*Aton Chekhov

A Catastrophe

I remember grasshoppers

Which backed up spring

Narrow little things

Made so by design

No time now

To call in

A future

If I were to write an orange poem,
it would have to be ridiculous.

It would have to be absurd
like a strawberry inside a grape.

The poem should be about de-creation,
or the minds retreat.

It should point to the highest point
of human imperfection.

It must be poorly written - weak;
full of artifice and deceit.

It would have to be hollow:
A body stepping out of its soul,

which reduced by the sum of its parts,
winds up as an orange smear;

which eventually torches its own intent.

I of the silences
sing dirges

I try and comfort the
enraged earth

with flowers

run with
dog
in his dream

I pretend
I am

a fox
no one can kill

Fish ripple with
chemical supplies

but my mountain
is waiting

or is my heart
only a wish bone?

The Zombie Apocalypse

The sky is falling after all.
Chicken Little was a wizard

who should have been heard
before it was too late.

Most of us are not heard.
We write in the margins of the page,

Ask about the new moon
or if there's bread upon the shelf.

My heart listens behind closed doors:
Eternity is a spasm in a Petri dish.

We want to be heard - count for something
now that the sky has gone.

Zombie Apocalypse 2

There is a lady here with strange
hair.
She used to be kept up.

Worries were singular
then.
Not so foul.

We were not
assigned
to such a low place

In the family
of
heavens.

There were no
parades
of sorrow then.

No rendering apparatus
with
license to harm.

Loneliness of a Mad Women

I left something important at your house.
Was it a ring?   The shadow of a doubt?

Upright things have gone.

My turtle pond with its colored rocks.
Points of reference where I could safely disembark.

Real things have gone.

My children's voices—the uproar of their ways:
And the exact way you buttered your toast.

Now, ghost lovers divide and become menacing.
Over and over again thoughts take away the Zen moment.

I gather the furniture into enclaves of solidarity.
Turn a deaf ear to trenchant cries for other voices

other eyes.

Were you mine or were you not?

You pressured me to buy a box of apricots.
Now you don't.

Is it better to alive seven days a week
or only on one good day?

Should I follow my children's pain?
Carry its full weight? Or shake my fist in their back yard?

Is there a God in Pick and Save?
Or only some kind of agitation.

Now What?

I say hi!

Old sperm dancer:
Old iron rod.

Hi! On this another day.
How are we going?

What! You're not signed up
for the expedition?

What! You are grumbly
and feel the cold?

Old deaths resurface?
Came out of their solid flesh
and you provoked them?

All along we knew.
But certain considerations
helped keep it away.

Now what?

Backwards To Armageddon

HERBERTO PADILLA

When my country fell,
and wisdom rode the back of clowns:

I could not become a flower. I could not become the rain.

I tried to harvest the wind but I was short handed
and now in a trying time, I am adrift.

In trying times you need backups; lively colors and strong legs.
You need sound—devices to hear silence.
Print outs for sing-a-longs.

In trying times you need to see the bright side of life,
because to see horror, one startled eye is enough."

Before red, white and blue became incendiary colors;
I was a hands—off person.

A persona non-grata, if you will.
   A gentle wind, a small portfolio.

     Then

I came across a pair of massive wings:
    Florescent and timed to kill.

They loosed hate upon us. They loosed their dark intent.
Hope trembled and tried to run.

I was fluent in outrage, so I shouted;

Let the truth tellers be heard. Let the hurt ones rise victorious.
Silly to walk on water—but you had to try.

The Sufferings

Hello Sofia!

Valentines, poet of the deep,
called you wisdom,

as you made the world
from pieces of yourself.

I tell the dark how all things
came about through suffering

and that I am not afraid.

But the dark snickers and
and makes me afraid again.

I tell water
this fable of Sofia by Valentines,

poet of the real
and water shows me what water is.

Horse Flies

I send search lights into this house of change.

Or I sit in a horse trailer, imaging miracles.

Sometimes I turn into a small God.

> Then

I weep, for the small contorted universe.

Hours

These lavender hours are like turning fruit.

Flattened out like old people's shoes,
stored too long from the idea

that more life is better then less life.

Everywhere grifters and spoilers
trespass over stars and everything

that happened as though they owned time
I suppose they do.

I called in to cancel the hours.
But by then the stars were black.

I want to replace anything that is not young
even all I learned,

as I can't remember what it was.

Also

I should have been careful of what I loved.

Affliction

This is a love poem and a poem about loss.
It's a mother and son poem.

It's a poem about bridges, dreams, courage.
And about the golden monkey, that hobbled the dream.

God's mother and father had looked over the dream.
They saw that it took courage.

Do you still have it? the dream, the bridge, the courage?
Even in a pinched sort of way?

Did the bridge break its promise? Not at all.
We built our house on the bridge, instead of just crossing it.

Life is a bridge, cross it
but build no house upon it.

The Pulmonologist

I appreciate you over most in this fierce and fettered time.

You are both gathered and expansive, sword and shield,
poised and still.

You come with a night light and a box of tools.

I visit you between schedules.
Between riptides of the unknown, in or out of necessity.

Your name is Sara, the old name: Meaning Princess,
Noble women.

You are also an outrigger in an urgent season,
seeking to cull—that living flower.

Part II

Mr. Death

and what i want to know is
*how do you like your blueeyed boy Mr. Death**

            the one
I had begged you to spare?

Why did you throw my pearls away?
            Can't you do anything right?

Now that you've got him, discourage his flawed myths.
Sing him a song. Quench the thirst in his Soul.

Learn about primordial love. The rending of source.

The God of Abraham, Isaac, and Jacob
            ask you to bring him back.
You Mr. Death.
            You, who have no eyes.

*see end notes

Heavy fate
for cow and calf.

Bird too
with stilled wing.

Appalling hours
cover the art of you.

Perhaps
I can spring you loose:

Pretend
you are a fox.

You are like bird.
Indistinct/silenced.

Boat Men (For A Son)

Recent skirmishes in the hearts eye leave me disordered.
Grief is kindling on a dry floor: The logic of the unendurable:

And a dimension of self that exceeds the stratosphere.
Every wall I lean against, falls down.

Your being, was the hope for which I've trained my pulses.

 But last night, in my strong and perfect dream,
ancient boat men ferried me to higher ground.

I'll look for you there my darling. You <u>must</u> be there.

*Failing to fetch me at first keep encouraged, Missing me one place
search another, I stop somewhere waiting for you.**

* see end notes

Stricken!

In my dream I asked about you.
Someone said you were dancing.

I wanted to be in the dance.
I wanted to bivouac with toy soldiers.

Or sleep forever—just to dream
that life came back.

What was this death they said you had?

My Son! My Son!

Call for the messenger.
Call for the day when you first came.

Where Is Your Mind?

I don't understand.
Where will your ideas be?

Where are they now?

Where is your walk—your hope?
What about the things you had to do?

You always ate fast as though you had no time.
But your ideas were resting places—cathartic.

You brought far-away universes into view.
so we could see them—here on the ground.

We knew these giants that lived in your mind,
Where is your mind?

It's absence is my undoing,

For Michael: 1956-2020

The unbearable cannot be bourn.

The deepest logic is a scream.

I stand here beside myself, screaming.

Oh Absalom, my son, my son! It was a joy to meet you.

You were the bedrock of my salty cause.

It's imperative that you call home.

The deepest logic is love.

Inside Covid

You have gone. You and I went seven times deep.
What seeded life has faltered.

Where are you now in the Raven high sky?
In the downing of the indifferent rain?

I kept all your garden tools handy. Ready for your garden.
I kept the remnants of a fire going.

I kept my own death hidden.
Grief is music at the bottom of a lake.

But I had a moment of great peace
I thought *that* peace, might have belonged to you.

I have been parsed into a knot. Slowed to a stop.

That which I feared has come upon me.*

* see end notes

Black Hole

I think I once made plans. Breakaway decisions:
I covered some ground.

Now, a vast desolation confounds reason.
The heart files a claim.

The black hole won't allow questions.
The black hole that is my silence, strikes the answer.

You ate. You had a phone number.
You slept on your side with your sleep apnea machine.

You were more than the sky.
What about all of that? I ask.

My wrath curls and foams down the sweaty street.
My meekness is only cover.

My Own

I am mother, wearing warm socks
in a sun-baked year.

Following life's protocols,
Parsing the light, with its dark tones.

We rode side-saddle for sixty-three years.
You said: *Hi mom; hi mom; hi mom.*

Now I am copious with sound bites
from another world.

Now I grieve.
Now I am crossing water, boatless and stricken.

After Your Death

I live inside an aquarium with unspeakably dumb fish.

I am a wall in anyone's house.

I have changed into a random persona, deemed unfit.

I have interrupted my heart beat.

Torn the pages from my everyday.

I jump-start each hour. Shop for a heaven.

Things to talk about belonged to long ago.

I've been changed by an archaic knowing,

but set adrift in an ordinary sea.

Grief Work

If everyone would pool their strength and lend me a little,
I would be grateful.

I would be alive again, be on my own ground.
Now this is what I know.

You had a phone number and plans for improvement.

You said, *Hi Mom, I can't talk now, I'll get back.*
You said, *Hi mom*; You said, *Hi mom,* for sixty years:

One hundred years: Said it forever.
You had good clothes and a phone number.

Freud called this *"grief work"*. What happens after the work?
Do I get get a bouquet of Chrysanthemum's?

My whelp—my issue.
My army of one.

My son, my mourn, my thorn.
My pup, my underground.

My holy craft.
My brilliant star.

My coming and going.
My underneath. My yearling.

I hurt and hurt. All hurt.

Sacrificial Lamb

And here is the tail end of it.

Without *time* in the way, I can see more clearly.

You always had to fit your large body
into small places. Also your larger mind.

You always had to do that.

Early wounds turned you into a rogue wanderer.

I am responsible.
I lived in a place of zeros on capsized ground.

Your great was vast, so I charge myself with genocide.

Having charged myself, I am inconsolable.

To You

O.K. I'll hand you over
give
you up to the sky

Send you full force
from this
jaundiced land

Where everything was
mostly
attitude born from lament

Out of synch
with
any Spring

It will be a different
sky
when I with quickened heart

And plangent eye
deed you
back to the beginning.

Michael

I understand death better.
I understand that the burning candle

has nothing
to do with his voice and his hope.

That the wreath
hung for him is only an object.

And that my need has nowhere to go.
That I can't keep him in any shape or form.

And that memory is only a sleight of hand
to which grief clings.

My darling: Are you gone? Where are your friends?

You were in my womb for 64 years.
I sense myself as missing.

I am a missing person with an empty womb.
Or perhaps I am the sky before daybreak.

In Time

When words are spears, I cringe.

He's in a better place.
You have to take care of yourself.
He's at peace."

He should not be at peace. He should be near his phone,
or on his computer. He needs to be - just getting along;

or pondering the mix of all things: The love of good itself,
while his mind flits from symbol to symbol.

In time butter will turn back to cream.
Meanwhile to live (which is evil spelled backward) I cannot do.

I am congealed minutiae saying long dry prayers,
which is like sipping candle wax through a straw.

When words are spears I hold the phone away.
No one is the wiser.

There was never a whole—a fullness maybe.

Emptiness is a fullness with silence.

Silence is a Mockingbird.

Regret is the light's whimper—the dark's door.

The rain and sun are my cousins.

The rain is Gods hair.

We were both lessons we could not learn.

I remember when you were called sweet a bird,

passenger or tall man in green.

I did not hoard minutes then

And you were a great heart with a forward call.

Now I sit under the tree of your birth.

and in my debt, sorrow and duty mix,

in the thin song of being:

In the penurious song of waste.

Fragments

You were the question that harpooned my sleep.

I could not sever your roll-over cause
and you rode your dark horse into the night.

Passages from great books and explanations did no good.
The brow was sickly damp from viral outcomes.

I'll write to soften the fetters of this grief.
Write to hone it down.

Bend it into a fragment of manageable outcome.

*These fragments I have shored against my ruins.**

Now I am a person of questionable regard.
Your life was in me. Without you I am only a part.

Christ!

Your breath was everything to me.

*see end notes

Bankrupt

Colors that I do not see anymore
candle my solitude.

Your missing colors disturb the
silence of all the

Saturdays and days that
have no sound.

You have scared
the ground of my intention.

But you will never be a
faded
tattoo on my hand.

Your light
made a calendar for days.

Life was not the tail-end
of some laconic prayer

where melancholy threw
It's weight against will

and days refused to
end their fast.

Measured Time

The mean pinch of measured time
was embedded in your face.

For me, the best thing now
is coping with the worst thing.

Just to ask you darling
from the root of my being.

Where are your resources?
Where is heaven?

What did you love as a child, that you need now?

*Full fathom five thy father lies. Those were pearls that were his eyes**

* see endnotes

Two Months Exactly

I am trying to find Michael.
My being is always searching.

Reading or washing, etc., etc.,
I am always aware that Michael must come back.

I am not exactly real anymore, because he was
added unto me and he has gone.

It is so cold today: January 29, 2021. Two months
without him.

He was added unto me. Without him I am
small and opaque. I cannot arrive nor depart.

I'll call you and when,

I hear your real voice in real time,

I'll say: Wonderful! Wonderful! Wonderful!

I thought that life had stopped.

You'll say: *Mom, stop it.*

Everywhere, flowers will bloom.

A Worthless Dream

When you entered the
terrible gate of time,

I changed your name
from son on the morning grass—

to blocked cargo.

I put you into the beat
of my heart.

My own name changed
from tides or small believer

to woman having dinner
on a paper tray.

Fly On My Sweet Angel

You left with no last word or glance,
so I could not hear the tone of your departure

which I needed to hear
to part the way for my own coming and going.

Where will you be with your smiles, thoughts
and those great loops of feelings?

Perhaps there is rebirth, a softening of hard luck,
or further appeals, in the hidden cannons of tomorrow.

*Fly on my sweet angel.**

* see end notes

Covid Story

I am a phantom with phantom eyes. I borrowed the
remnants of a former self and pantomime yesterday.

But what they told me was wrong. You cannot be dead.
Some border is just obscured, relocated or prolapsed.

You were a larger than your sum. An original design.
You were an light arc within a luminate sky.

Now, real things and sustaining circles are gone.
In accustomed cant, medical providers (sticky with pantomime)
ask if I want to die as well?

I would be a fool to answer truthfully.

Hoarfrost

This poem is for the unforgiving void.

I am in the void, non-reflective and unclaimed,
waiting for you.

Life brushes against me like hoarfrost.
It is broken and I am insolvent.

You <u>were</u> and now you're <u>not</u>. I need to know you are,

as I cannot pay the piper for past debt
nor begin to reference your vast dimension.

Answering The Emptiness

When you died God left too.
Even before, prayers were like dead wires.

When God left
taking the Song of Songs, and all things in between,

I left in my own way, leaving a furled wing;
Bits of a before.

Here in the large chair,

I scan days for something significant
and lightly colored.

For a re-trial, if you will.

I had said, this prayer poem would be for myself only.
But I can't keep this promise on the page.

Dry Sockets

We struggled for light in our box of hearts;
brave in the cuticle of days.

We twisted the rain into a sculpture
to make it last.

We turned the sun into a playful god.

Without you, nothing starts to begin.
Without you, days push.

I do not remember you, so much as breathe you,
in and out of memory, and everywhere you're gone, I weep.

Sticks And Ashes

I knew Sebelsky
who had horses

I used to ride
in the deep valley

in the hills
where it was dry.

I carried your
promise inside me.

It was a sermon
I did not hear.

Now age seeps through me
and steals my origins.

Now I am
a blocked thoroughfare;

a pile
of leftovers;

a splintered moment;
a cup of rain

I offer salutations
to a far away god

and live by
the heave of

the will.

Shadow Drawing

The truth is simple,
like water or sleep.

Your face without pain,
or glass and things put in rows.

Desire makes things complicated.

Truth is clean fingernails and
dirty fingernails.

A handrail, silence or fear.

The truth is simple,
like silence or water.

Dirge With No Music

His mother was a dreamer in the viscous wasteland,
searching for possibility.

But now all she could see were dead crickets,
dirty socks and no buckets of rainwater.

Death changes the perspective.
Truth and lies become footnotes.

What about a reversal in time? The mother begged?
What about the long-term value of his heart?

Disinherit the heart?
Certainly the ears, and the eyes that saw too much.

But the heart? That once knew the in-between.

Don't worry, said my Soul to the emptiness.
A seam in the dark will open. Light will flood in.

I'll see your face in the emptiness
sunning itself on the outskirts of memory.

I'll chase your silhouette
in the unplumbed realm of sleep.

You were a visionary in the house of knowing
and should have been first in line.

But I cannot do life, without its bread and butter.
I cannot do life without you:

And all my thoughts are like water in the wind.

Bereft

My son is gone. My child is gone.

And I Am

A circle with knives turned inward.

I know that I cannot live as the only I am
an unmistakable me. You made me

myself

with your fierce heartbeat.

Judas

I was a bread winner. I was a kissing expert.
But I rolled out of those things.

And before you could say, *Jack Robinson*!

I began to smell like cinnamon or old ivory.
Sometimes my breath smelled sour.

When you were with me, you said this wouldn't happen.
You said I would always be.

That sour breath would sweeten.
That was what I thought you said.

I thought we would always have plans.
I had your word. I held your hand.

Names For A May Child

Call me when hope
is a bang and not a whimper
when you are all along right
and up with the wind.

Call me,
in the middle of nothing much.

I'd like to name you
propitious fellow or he

who walks straight on a crooked line,
or window, so you can look out.

Even something hand me down
like rain, as it is Gods music.

But in a country of faces, I cannot find you.
Though you were the color of creation.

Your name was Michael.
You were a quotient in a random light.

My Children

We were in that neighborhood
when I was twice as young and

there was summer rain.

I gave a party, like Mrs. Dalloway. *
But only Angels came—the men

in brown suits and derby hats;
the women in forties style dresses.

Even now, I hear them
restraining the dark with their

distant wings, tearing the curtained Spirit down

to let light in.

All night I hear them
and I want to tell the Angles that my son is dead;

that I would have given him my skin and
my lungs.

Why can't he come back? I'd ask them.
He was all of it.

* see endnotes

Flawed Mother

your wound did not heal.
It became the centerpiece of a grim sonata.

I loved you;

You could not hear this refrain, especially on your winter walk.

Cancel the stagnant culture of the heart.
Instead, set rivers on fire.

The grandmother and the great, great grandmother,
she of the Jewish Ashkenazim were also wounded:

and cloud - covered.

But the moments clutch and are profoundly withholding.

The Incorruptible

There is urgency. Some sort of struggle
for coherence.

Also for release.

Linen dresses in sky colors are only a pretext.
Something is un-channeled, out of reach.

It is not possible
to render anything you touched obsolete.

Or to keep you with me—body and Soul.

A Death

Is there something more?
as

the present
is a pity

with medicated days
and myopic eyes.

I am a lump of coal.
I am a missing person,

groping for certitude.

Your death!
has etched itself into my ruins.*

*see endnotes

A Cry

My isle of mourning widens.

The concussion was severe.

Now I am two people, on an incoherent string of time.

A serge of deaths: (The report said)
Nigeria had less death.
Dr. Joshi is still shuttling between hospitals.
Why Nigeria? They said.

Why my son? I said.
I shuttle between defected Gods.

A Story

I'll come in summer when the ground is good.
I'll come in spring,
trafficked in from a different planet.

Or I'll come in fall, in a change of clothes.
I'll call you through the whistling shrine
of an old heart and a potted grief.

But I should come in winter
the season which knows me best.
I should come on the wings of the White Owl.

But drastic outcomes have aged me.
I follow the habits of the Ground Hog.

Even so, I'll come. Believing I'll find you.

I need to find the truth behind the grave.
I need to find you!

Not huddled in the grasses of the moon
or in some shuttered passageway,

but in the light where I can see you
transformed from servant into sovereign.

When you were an infant, a clinging vine.
I was a wholehearted being.

Now I am a small shell. A broken drum.

I want to leave this drafty runway,
find the messenger with his high-born fruit.

I must find you!

And life must have asked death for something you could keep.
Maybe it was everything. Maybe it was just the rain.

A Premier 83rd Birthday

I've set the table   as though

guests were coming.   As though

there were no Covid, chemical supplies
or the bewilderment of death   As though

I was a child again on a good day.

I've set the table with blue dinner ware,   as though

you were coming.   As though

I were young again and not
cavorting with either saints or bargain hunters;

Neither an up-start nor a holy fool,
full of misinformation.   As though

I were a queen in my pajamas,
waiting for you.

Spilled Dancer

This poem is about arms, legs, parts, etc., etc.,

falling or spilling over.

It is about the

supine spine

in tumble dry knots.

I am

a spilled dancer,

a failed sermon

a stilled other.

Harmony

Everything here is understated.
There is more down the road

where rain

changes into music
and all the prayers gather

in gratitude.

They sing in the early dawn's dark
of the supernatural color of wet earth

or a coming reprieve.

page 17 *Being Eclipsed*
*In the cities the bells rang all day long: everyone was being summoned, but
no one knew who was summoning them or why**
—Fyodor Dostoevsky, *Crime and Punishment*, 1866
  (trans. Richard Pevear & Larissa Volokhonsky)

page 53 *Mr. Death*
and what i want to know is how do you like your blueeyed boy, Mr. Death
—ee cummings

page 55 *Boat Men (For A Son)*
*Failing to fetch me at first keep encouraged, Missing me one place search
another, I stop somewhere waiting for you. **
—Walt Whitman, *Song of Myself, 52,* 1855

page 59 *Inside Covid*
*That which I feared has come upon me. **
The Book of Job, Chapter 3, Verse 25, Bible, King James 2000

page 70 *Fragments*
*These fragments I have shored against my ruins**
—T.S. Eliot, *Waste Land,* (Final Stanza), Line 430

page 72 *Measured Time*
*Full fathom five they father lies. Those were pearls that were his eyes.**
—William Shakespeare, *The Tempest,* (Ariel's song) Act I, Sc. II

page 76 *Angel*
*Fly on, my sweet angel. **
Song by Jimi Hendrix; album *The Cry of Love,* 1971

page 88 *My Children*
**Mrs. Dalloway* is a novel by Virginia Woolf (1882-1941). It is one
of Woolf's best-known novels. Published by Hogarth Press May 14,
1925.

page 91 *A Death*
*has etched itself into my ruins**
—T.S. Eliot

About the Author

Gail Gauldin Moore was a voiceless poet all of her life, having had writer's block for over fifty years. She finally starting writing after a vision of a strange animal emerged from a cave and began shaking off its wool.

She was a licensed therapist for over thirty years, received a certificate in Theological Studies from Sewanee, University of the South, and was an adjunct professor for The University of La Verne.

She thinks poetry should strive to remain what it was once thought to be, "the highest of the literary arts" and likes this summation of the poetic process by Galway Kinnell:

> "On some hill of despair
> the bonfire you kindle
> can light the great sky;
> though it is true of course,
> that to make it burn,
> you have to throw yourself in."